Center and Periphery

 PARK BOOKS

Five Houses by Mikael Bergquist

Photography by Mikael Olsson and Åke E:son Lindman

The Comfort of the Archipelago 4
House for Two Artists 10
House T 22
House Melvin 26
Red House 36
Holiday Home 42
Center and Periphery 50
Drawings 58

The Comfort of the Archipelago

Charlotte von Moos

In today's digitized reality, it is easy to assume our cultures are identical. The definition of comfort, such an inherent part of inhabiting architecture, does indeed have the potential to reveal these differences. The five wooden houses by Mikael Bergquist, built outside Stockholm between 2005 and 2020, may provide certain clues that allow us to reflect on the presumptive sameness put forward by the philosopher Susan Neiman:

> Global capitalism has reduced cultural contrasts, but it hasn't erased them.[1]

Some of these houses can be reached from Stockholm by car, while others are more remote and require a ferry trip. But all of them relate to a specifically Swedish mode of living in and with the land and the littoral that has become even more distinct in recent years. The subtle processes of infantilization in most nontotalitarian societies are considerable, and idealize endless adolescence, "giving us comfort through an endless range of toys."[2] Rem Koolhaas rightly claims that Americans have become "obsessed with comfort".[3] Once comfort is dependent on size and technologies such as climate control and constant digital connection, it becomes independent of its location. One marker of this trend is the luxury SUVs like the Cadillac Escalade—floating living rooms full of tech-enabled comforts.[4]

In Sweden, though, it took a teenage climate activist, namely Greta Thunberg, to change the mindset of many of its inhabitants, resulting in "flight shaming," a decrease in domestic air travel, and a renewed interest in weekend houses across and beyond the Stockholm Archipelago (further enhanced by the pandemic), suggesting that the attitude towards both restlessness and comfort had been revised. One wonders whether these calls for action were heeded more here than elsewhere because Sweden has a more profound relationship with its land: such a vast country with few inhabitants.[5]

Sweden's location at the periphery of Europe, its littoral condition, and its intense climate may have informed its people's deep, cyclical connection with geography, as captured so elegantly by Lars Lerup:

> The summers in this theater are short but flooded in a relentless light that is so intense, demanding, and invasive that the night is erased—only to return and settle in for months to come.[6]

It is in this tidal zone of "where liquid meets solid"[7] that Bergquist's houses stand so axiomatically, often replacing existing farmhouses and reflecting on some of architecture's most fundamental themes: the hut, the roof, the window, the chimney, the garden. The work is radical in its own way, embracing an American interpretation of "the ordinary" (via Venturi's "gentle manifesto,"[8] which idiosyncratically focused on a formalist interpretation of specific aspects of the architecture of Western Europe) alongside Jasper Morrison's "super normal"[9] in its attitude toward both expression and construction, Swedish style.

Red House, for example, with its brilliantly red wooden façade, responds to traditional Swedish tropes by way of Jan Gezelius' Villa Drake (Borlänge, 1968–70). The house's simple exterior form, its appearance shrunk by the dark Falu red that traditionally symbolized Swedish pastoral life and here pays respect to the near pinewood forest, contrasts with its strikingly bright, white-painted wood interior that magnifies all the spaces. This effect is reinforced by windows that are strategically placed to connect to different facets of the garden's topography, trees, and plants. The round window on the gallery level, a nod to Josef Frank's Villa Beer (Vienna, 1920), permits sophisticatedly framed views of the trees and the sky. In contrast, the large cubic fireplace grounds the cabin more primordially to its soil.

In House Melvin, the wooden façade is left raw, while only the window frames are elegantly painted white like a rural mirage of Josef Frank's Villa Claesson (Falsterbo, 1924–27). On each side of the façade, a glazed door element protrudes slightly from the main volume to allow more unexpected viewing angles. Another large round window is almost hidden away, framing the littoral shrubs. This is where the theme of the wood deck emerges: these decks create a light, planar threshold between the house and garden in an accidental, beachlike manner, extending the interior into the outdoors and reflecting the sky back into the house, yet with respectfully minimal groundwork.

The small house on Ljusterö combines two tracts under one roof, like some farmhouses. The main house is divided from the children's rooms by an arched exterior hallway, generating a careful tension of symmetry and asymmetry in the unassuming façades. The ever-present littoral landscape makes the rooms and bathrooms seem tiny but comfortable.

With its interior fully clad in plywood, the house on Nämdö stands apart, its three-dimensional details akin to the precision of Donald Judd's sculptures in the same material. Yet, in a wink to the Swedish Romantic style of

Ragnar Östberg—one is reminded of his use of salvaged components for the 1912 Stockholm City Hall[10]—this wooden composition is juxtaposed with a huge baroque tiled oven that brings the urban sophistication of Stockholm to this remote island.

With its long and narrow proportions, at first glance the house on Ornö resembles a manufactured trailer home. Likewise, its location within the forest clearing initially gives the impression of it having landed by accident, and of being temporarily affixed to the ground by nothing more than another light wooden deck. It calls to mind Josef Frank's thoughts on accidentism:

> Every place in which we feel "comfortable"—rooms, streets, and cities—has originated by chance.[11]

Yes, the dark wood façade, blending with the pine tree trunks, responds to this place's specificity. However, the crisp clarity of the symmetrical plan and façades make this project more of a device to measure and better understand the landscape than a house.

In its own way, each of Bergquist's five wooden houses suggests an unpretentious way of living on the littoral. His designs are tempered by the unique locality of his native Sweden. Surprisingly, in that relationship, they may be more closely related to Glenn Murcutt's outback houses than Central European ancestors (and he, like Bergquist, works alone).

His is an architecture of place, architecture that responds to the landscape and climate. His houses are fine tuned to the land and the weather.[12]

Resembling Murcutt's design attitude both in its primeval proportions and precise simplicity realized as a sturdier wooden construction to respond to the harsh littoral conditions, Bergquist's architecture incorporates a hopeful, peaceful, and more aware Swedish way of life. With its singular definition of comfort, it resists the restlessness of contemporary living. The main protagonist here invariably remains the archipelago, with all its mysteries and deeper truths.

1 Susan Neiman, *Why Grow Up? Subversive Thoughts for an Infantile Age*, New York: Farrar, Straus, and Giroux, 2014, p. 162.

2 Ibid., p. 39.

3 Rem Koolhaas, "Workspace: Challenge vs. Comfort," lecture, Cannes Lions, June 20, 2013.

4 Farhad Manjoo, "Help. I've Fallen for that Cadillac Escalade," *New York Times*, February 4, 2022.

5 Sweden's population density is one of the lowest in Europe, with 24 people per square kilometer; Switzerland, in comparison, has 213 people in the same area, a stressful density that generates a sense of restlessness.

6 Lars Lerup, *The Life and Death of Objects: Autobiography of a Design Projec*t, Basel: Birkhäuser, 2022, p. 15.

7 Ibid., p.10.

8 Robert Venturi*, Complexity and Contradiction in Architecture*, Museum of Modern Art Papers on Architecture, 1966.

9 Jasper Morrison and Naoto Fukasawa, *Super Normal*, Zurich: Lars Müller Publishers, 2006.

10 Ákos Moravánsky, "Circular materiality—key concepts in ecological construction," in *Re-Use in Construction: A Compendium of Circular Architecture*, Zurich: Park Books, 2022, p. 21.

11 Josef Frank, "Accidentism," in *Form*, 54 (1958), pp. 161–166.

12 2002 Pritzker Prize, jury citation.

House for Two Artists
Nämdö
2020

House T
Ornö
2022

House Melvin
Hamburgsund
2012

Red House Sparreholm 2002

Holiday Home
Ljusterö
2018

Center and Periphery

Mikael Bergquist

First, two short digressions: one about music and one, which I encountered recently, about clothing. Although they have little to do with architecture directly, curiously they touch on the themes of this text as well as on my own ambitions as an architect.

The late American art critic Dave Hickey wrote of his favorite record, *Chet Baker Sings*:

> I played it all the time, morning and night, and it spoke to me then of a special kind of elegiac cool; it dispensed with all pretension to musical heroism without repudiating the idea of heroism itself [...].[1]

Baker sings American jazz standards on the album, which was recorded at the end of the 1950s. His performance is entirely free from the cult of originality and masculine self-expression; he plays and sings with neither vibrato nor powerful statements. "In contemporary terms," Hickey added:

> Baker does not so much "perform" these songs as "simulate" them—appropriating their complete content to his own intentions while leaving the song itself with its formal integrity unmolested.[2]

The other text is an amusing article in the magazine *Fantastic Man* about the French writer Benoît Duteurtre, describing the style négligé mode of dress. It is "a dazzling and strictly French-only mix of good taste, quality-brand clothing, shabby maintenance and just-right unfashionability."[3] This deliberate unawareness of dress, or style négligé, exists neither in

Anglo-Saxon countries, where people think that clothing is an unambiguous language of the market, nor in wholly Latin countries, which find their rhetoric in the perfection of exaggeration. No one can teach it because its strategies are personal, and also because those who practice it refuse to admit that they do so.

Sweden is located on the periphery of Europe. It is a sparsely populated elongated country, large parts of which are covered by forest. Darkness falls early during the winter months, while summer is filled with daylight. Sweden has always been somewhat removed from the continent's major currents, which have reached us later than other places. The Swedish architect Jan Gezelius spoke of fruitful misunderstandings and the importance of Swedish poverty in interpreting international currents. We have always had a hard time dealing with the overflow. We have a long tradition of simple, robust, and economical solutions. Living and working on the periphery of Europe gives architects here a certain freedom. Swedish architecture in the last century and through to the present day contains a web of different directions and individuals. The two foremost Swedish architects of the twentieth century, Gunnar Asplund and Sigurd Lewerentz, both made highly personal and original versions of the arts and crafts style as well as their classical and modernist architecture. Gunnar Asplund was notable for his lightness and grace, Sigurd Lewerentz for his gravity. Think of Asplund's Woodland Chapel with its intimate scale, surrounded by tree trunks, and the comfort and elegance of its unexpected domed interior. This contrasts with Lewerentz's dry Lutheran interpretation of the same building type in Kvarnsveden's cemetery chapel, featuring an abject belfry that the church council voted to demolish shortly after

1. Gunnar Asplund, Woodland Chapel, Woodland Cemetery, Stockholm 1918–20
2. Sigurd Lewerentz, Pilgrim Chapel, Kvarnsveden Cemetery, Borlänge 1919–24
3. Swedish countryside cottage, Katrineholm, 1910

4

5

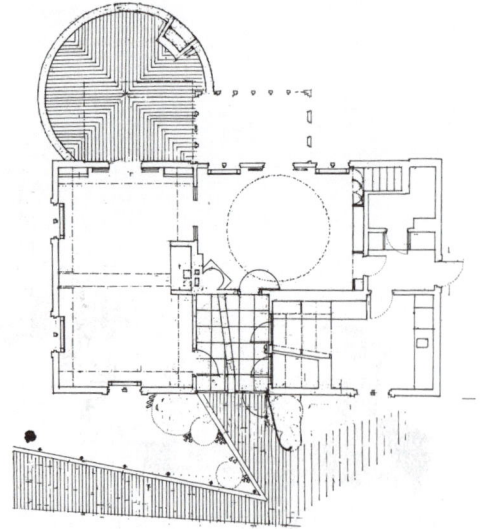

6

4. Jan Gezelius, Fiskarens hus [Fisherman's House], Böda, Öland, 1963
5. Klas Anshelm, Villa Oljelund, Tynnered, Göteborg, 1970–71
6. Peter Celsing, Villa Klockberga, Drottningholm, Stockholm, 1966–69

construction because it was deemed too ugly and simple.

In the 1960s and 1970s, personal versions of the small single-family house were created by various Swedish architects. Jan Gezelius made his characteristically horizontal, long, and narrow wooden houses with gabled roofs. Klas Anshelm's Villa Oljelund (1974) is clad in black-painted plywood with openable windows in red paint and fixed windows applied to the façade without proper frames, in a similar manner to Lewerentz. The original and simple detailing throughout the house includes a bathroom clad in plywood. Peter Celsing's own house, Villa Klockberga (1968), is a small, remodeled preexisting house. Celsing used it almost like a sketchbook for his larger commissions in the center of Stockholm. The small house is clad in black-painted sheet metal on the outside with brightly painted yellow windows, while on the inside it brings to mind Sir John Soane's Museum in London. It has been called the first postmodern Swedish villa.

Just a few generations back in time, most Swedes were small farmers who lived in the countryside. My own grandmother and grandfather came from these simple circumstances, and late in life they seized the opportunity to rent a cottage in the countryside as their holiday home. This red-painted house is still in the family today. Like so many other houses of its type, it has a straightforward simplicity, built in wood at the highest point of the plot. As a house it is economical, durable, and beautiful. The obvious proximity to nature and the mental image of the red-painted cabin lives on today.

Wood has always been a dominant material in smaller buildings. Although Sweden has a large forestry industry, wood-based construction has proved surprisingly conservative, but this is slowly changing. In recent years, new fire regulations have made it possible to build taller wooden buildings.

Today, various versions of the balloon frame are still the dominant technique for building small wooden houses. The frame is clad in different layers of material. The design is very much about detailing around the window openings, the eaves, the paneling of the façade, and the point at which the building meets the ground. Climate, rain, snow, and wind are of major concern, as well as the building's durability over time and its maintenance needs.

The five houses collected in this book are located at various rural locations in Sweden—three of them on islands in the archipelago outside Stockholm. A fourth is located in the countryside neighboring the fields of a local farmer, and the fifth is on the west coast of Sweden, exposed to salty winds and wet weather.

Gathering projects like this highlights the relative similarity between the houses, even though they were created over a period of nearly twenty years. In fact, the houses could almost be versions of the same building. I have always been interested in the everyday and the normal, as well as the way in which different materials are perceived and how they age and take on a patina. What has been central to all the projects is the sustained process of establishing a connection between the interior and the natural world that surrounds them. The ceiling height can differ in different parts of the house, giving a small house a bit of grandeur that can be combined with lower room heights for more intimate sections. In the House for Two Artists, the clients introduced me to the idea of installing an old fully functional tiled stove in the middle of the house. I was reluctant at first, which surprises me now that the house is finished and the stove is standing there, providing the living room with warmth and a certain interesting ambiguity.

I have a long-running interest in the Austrian–Swedish architect Josef Frank, not as a historical figure but as an architect with relevance today. I have written books on him, staged exhibitions, and recently renovated two of his villas in southern Sweden. At the end of his 1931 essay The House as Path and Place, Josef Frank gives a definition of modern architecture that I have always found very appealing, and a good guide when undertaking domestic architecture. He places it at the heart of the trivial, everyday domain, stating:

> Yet the rules for the good house as an ideal do not change in principle and have only to be looked at afresh. How does one enter a garden? What does the route look like from the gateway? What is the shape of an anteroom? How does one pass the cloakroom from the anteroom to reach the living room? How does the seating area relate to the door and the window? There are many questions like this which need to be answered, and the house consists of these elements. This is modern architecture.[4]

1 Dave Hickey, *Air Guitar: Essays on Art & Democracy*, Los Angeles: Art Issues Press, 1997, p. 75.

2 Ibid., p. 76.

3 Bruce Benderson, "Benoît Duteurtre: The Charming French Writer and the Dying Expertise of 'Style Négligé,'" *Fantastic Man*, 3 (2006), p. 81.

4 *Der Baumeister*, 29/8 (August 1931). English translation in *Josef Frank Writings*, Vol. 2, Vienna: Metro Verlag, 2012, p. 209.

Drawings

House for Two Artists
Nämdö, Stockholm Archipelago 2022

The simple form of this house is akin to traditional farmhouses in Sweden. It is situated on an island in the Stockholm Archipelago that can only be reached by boat.
   Although rather modest, the building affords family members and guests both social interaction and privacy.
   The outside of the house is clad in untreated solid materials that will age well and require virtually no maintenance.
   The interior is like a large piece of furniture, with its walls and ceilings clad in pine plywood. A fully functioning old tiled stove has been installed in the living room.

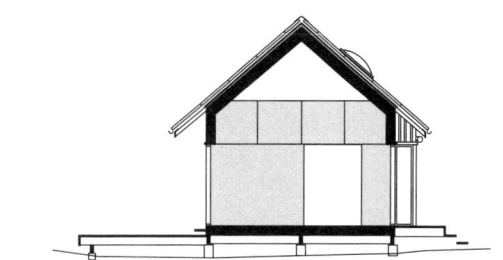

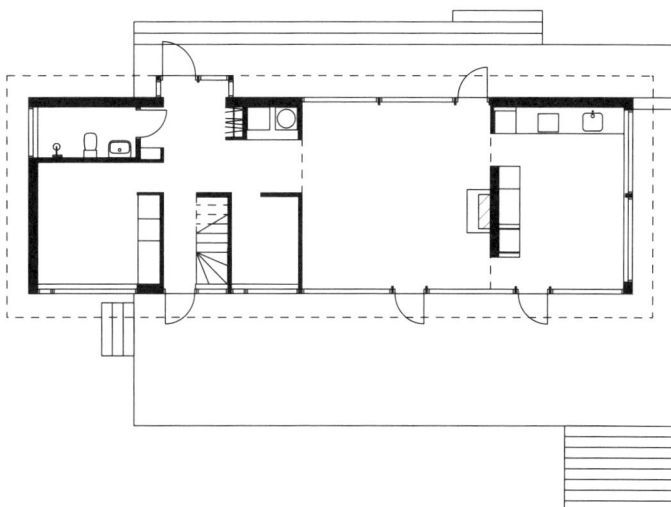

House T
Ornö, Stockholm Archipelago 2022

House T is situated near the water in the woods on a large island in the Stockholm Archipelago. The long house has two almost identical sections, with private rooms mirrored around the social spaces that contain the living room, dining room, and kitchen. Almost all the rooms have access to the outside.

The façade looking out onto the water has various different window types that relate to the inside of the house—a feature that gives the property a very special character.

Collaborator: Jan Anduaga

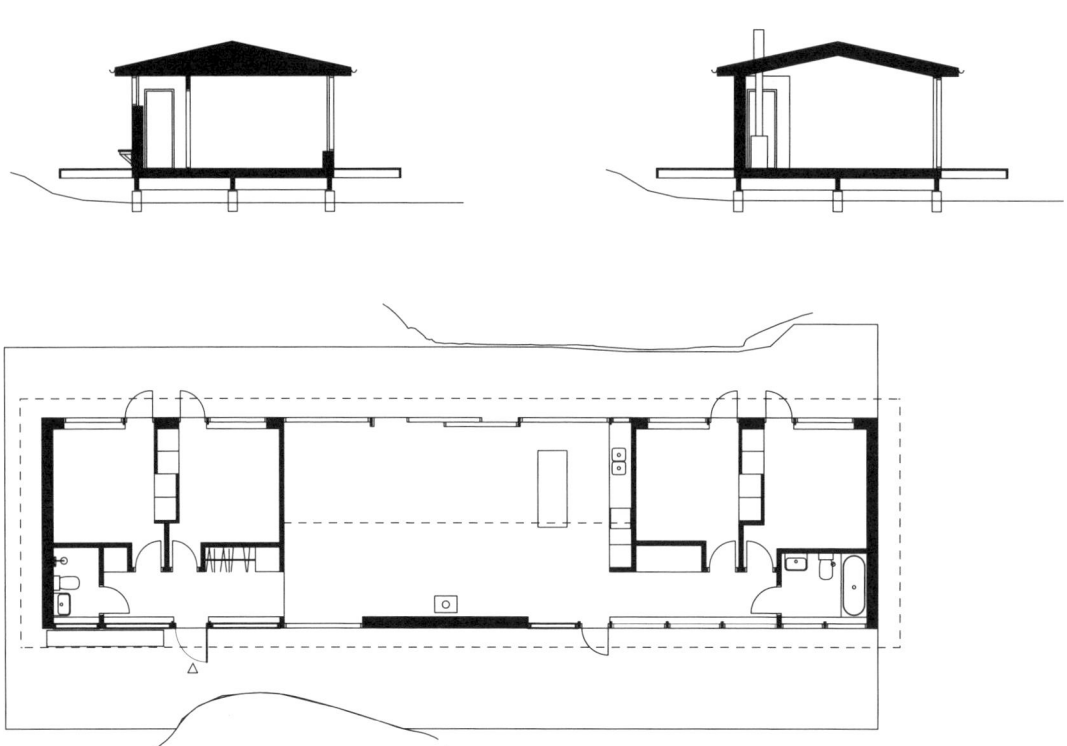

House Melvin
Hamburgsund, Bohuslän 2012

The living room can be opened up through the large sliding glass sections, turning it into an inside/outside room.
 The bedrooms and entrance hall are 2.15 meters high, while the combined living room is open to the ridge.
 A longitudinal steel beam enables the living room to remain an open space without columns or tie rods.

Landscape architect: Per Axelson

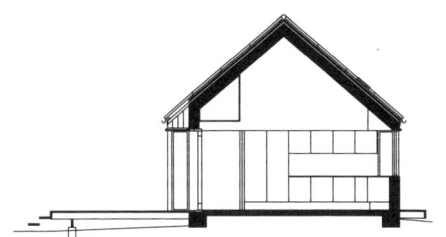
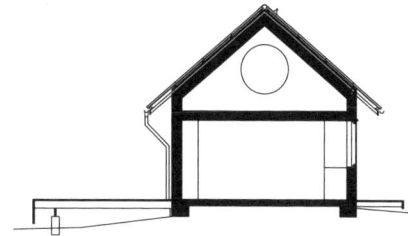
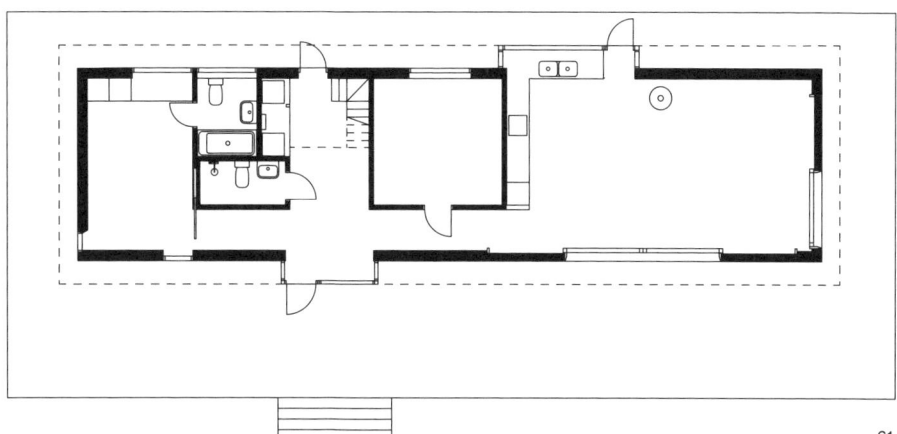

Red House
Sparreholm, Sörmland 2002

The house is located by Lake Båven, amidst an agricultural landscape in central Sweden. Its red color links it to the barns and utility buildings in the surrounding areas. A large fireplace faces the living room and screens off the kitchen. In the kitchen there is another fireplace and a wood stove. The loft on the upper floor receives daylight from two large round windows on each side of the cross.

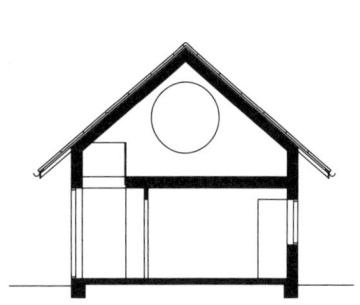
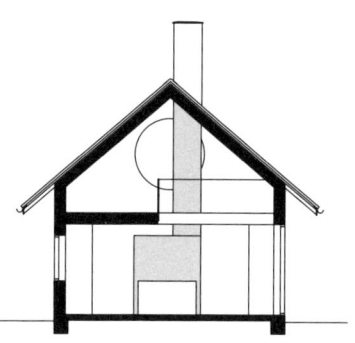
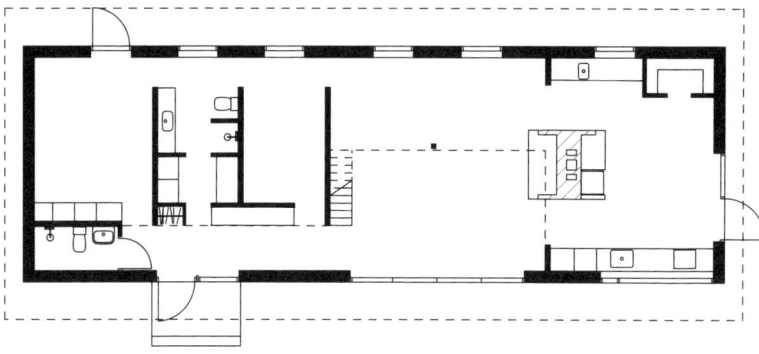

Holiday Home on Ljusterö, Stockholm Archipelago 2018

The house consists of two structures, a main building and a guest house, which are linked by a gable roof with an open passageway between them. The unfurnished attic of the guest house can be insulated and turned into additional rooms over time. The arched openings in conjunction with the large windows give the house a certain grandeur.

Collaborators: Emil Kedbrant, Dan Lindau

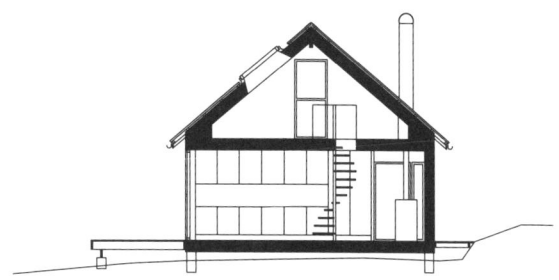

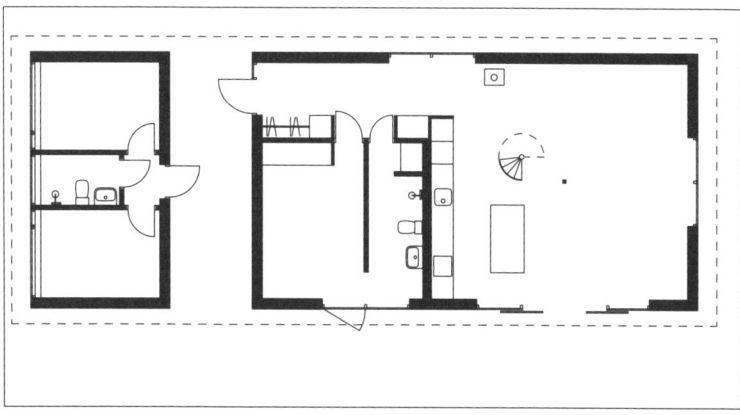

Authors: Charlotte von Moos, Mikael Bergquist
Copy Editing: Nicola Morris for Tradukas GbR
Proofreading: Colette Forder
Graphic Design: Daniel Bjugård, Stockholm
Typeface: Akzidens Grotesk
Paper: Munken Kristall, 150 g/m2
Printing and Binding: DZA Druckerei zu Altenburg, Thuringia

Thank you:
Charlotte von Moos, Miami, Daniel Bjugård, Stockholm, Maria Hedensjö Bergquist, Stockholm, Mikael Olsson, Stockholm, Thomas Kramer, Zurich

Image Credits:
All photos of House for Two Artists, House T, House Melvin by Mikael Olsson, Stockholm.

All photos of Red House, Holiday Home on Ljusterö by Åke E:son Lindman, Stockholm.

Pages 53–54:
1. C.G. Rosenberg, ArkDes, Stockholm
2. Unknown, ArkDes, Stockholm
3. Maria Hedensjö Bergquist
4. Sune Sundahl, ArkDes, Stockholm
5. Max Plunger, ArkDes, Stockholm
6. Arkitektur 9, 1989

All drawings M.B.A. Stockholm

© 2025 by Mikael Bergquist, Stockholm, and Park Books, Zurich
© 2025 for the texts, the authors

Park Books is being supported by the Federal Office of Culture with a general subsidy for the years 2021–2025.

All rights reserved; no part of this publication may be reproduced, stored in a retrieval system, or transmitted in any form or by any means, electronic, mechanical, photocopying, recording, or otherwise, without the prior written consent of the publisher.

Park Books
Niederdorfstrasse 54
8001 Zurich Switzerland
www.park-books.com

ISBN 978-3-03860-377-1